Angel
Book
A BABY LOSS JOURNAL

This book is dedicated to our
Sweet Julian + Ariella Luna
We love you to the moon and back

"No One Ever Wanted
Anything More Than I
Wanted you"

← - - - - - - - - - →

Unknown

DATE:

- Pregnancy test?
- How I felt?
- Who I told?

Dear Baby,

The day we found out about you…

"I carried you every second of your life and I will love you for every second of mine"

Unknown

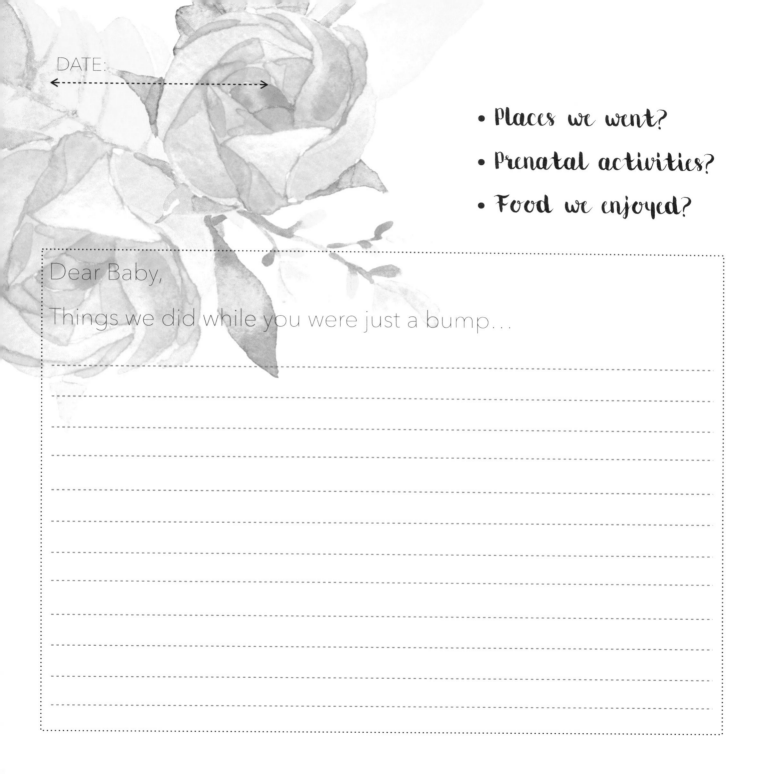

DATE:

- Places we went?
- Prenatal activities?
- Food we enjoyed?

Dear Baby,

Things we did while you were just a bump…

"Some say you are too painful to remember, I say you are too wonderful to forget"

Unknown

DATE: ←------------------→

- **Heart beat?**
- **Kicks?**
- **Ultrasound?**

Dear Baby,

My favorite memory of you is when...

"For it was not into my ear you whispered, but into my heart. It was not my lips you kissed, but my soul"

Judy Garland

YOUR NAME:

- Contenders?
- Meaning?
- Language?

Dear Baby,

The story of your name...

- -

- -

- -

- -

- -

- -

- -

- -

- -

- -

- -

"You are rooted deep within my soul. A part of me forever in the deepest depths of my heart there you are"

←------------------→

Jessi Snapp

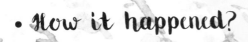

- How it happened?

- How I felt?

- Who was there?

Dear Baby,

The day I lost you...

_____

_____

_____

_____

_____

_____

_____

_____

_____

_____

"There is no footprint so small that it does not leave an imprint on this world"

Unknown

DATE:

Dear baby,

I remember you everyday by...

"I will always wonder who you would have been"

Unknown

DATE: <--------------------------------->

- 1.
- 2.
- 3.

Dear baby,

Three things I wish I knew about you are...

"Until we are together again, I will celebrate and honor you, because you made me a mother"

Unknown

DATE:

Dear baby,

One thing I wish you knew about me…

....
....
....
....
....
....
....
....
....
....
....

"How very softly you tiptoed into our world. Almost silently. Only a moment you stayed. But what an imprint your steps have left upon our hearts."

<------------------->

Dorothy Ferguson

- Dad?
- Brother?
- Sister?
- Pets?
- Granparets?

DATE:

Dear baby,

Let me tell you about your family…

"I am forever changed, you will not be forgotten."

Unknown

DATE:

- Act of Kindness?
- Donations?
- Tree planting?

Dear baby,

I will honor your angelversary by...

"Don't judge. You don't know what storm I've asked her to walk through"

Unknown

DATE: ←------------------→

Dear baby,

I am a stronger mother and individual now because…

....

....

....

....

....

....

....

....

....

....

....

Alice:

"How long is forever?"

White Rabbit:

"Sometimes just one second"

←------------------→

Lewis Carol

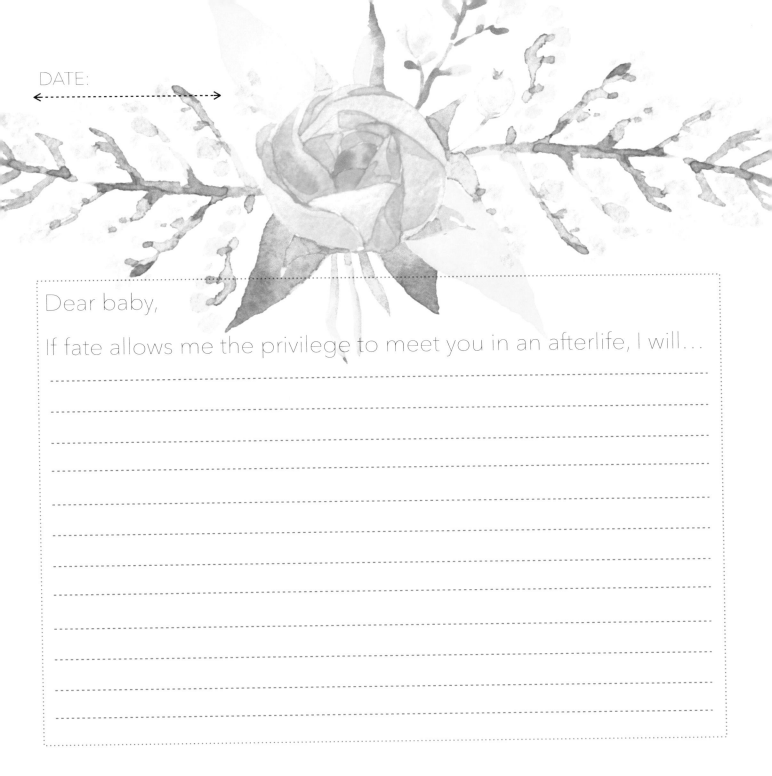

DATE:

Dear baby,

If fate allows me the privilege to meet you in an afterlife, I will…

....
....
....
....
....
....
....
....
....
....
....

AUTHOR'S NOTE

IT IS WITH THE DEEPEST LOVE AND AFFECTION THAT I HAVE CREATED A SERIES OF BABY LOSS JOURNALS. THIS JOURNAL IS MEANT TO HELP LOSS MAMAS CONNECT WITH HER BABY IN A MANNER THAT WILL ALSO HELP HEAL + INSPIRE HER GRIEVING HEART.

AFTER HAVING THE MOST BLISSFUL PREGNANCY WITH OUR FIRSTBORN, WE DECIDED ONE MORE WOULDN'T HURT. AT THIRTY-ONE WEEKS OUR BABY'S HEART STOPPED BEATING AND MY OWN HEART WAS SHATTERED AND TORN. ON NOV 6, 2015 WE HELD OUR BABY CLOSE AND SAID GOODBYE TO OUR SWEET JULIAN. WHILE SURVIVING THE WORST PAIN IN MY LIFE AND STRUGGLING THROUGH PARALYZING GRIEF, I BEGAN TO WRITE LETTERS TO MY BABY ON MY IPHONE. I THEN REALIZED THIS HELPED TREMENDOUSLY AND SOON LEARNED THROUGH ONLINE COMMUNITY SUPPORT THAT MANY OTHER MOTHERS WHO EXPERIENCED BABY LOSS THROUGH MISCARRIAGE OR STILLBIRTH, ALSO FOUND HEALING IN JOURNALING. AS I WALKED THE BABY ISLES AT THE BOOKSTORES, THERE WERE NO JOURNALS DEDICATED TO BABY LOSS AND NOTHING TO HONOR OUR BABIES' BRIEF LIVES AMONG THE ROWS OF PREGNANCY AND BABY MEMORY BOOKS. IF THERE WERE ANY BOOKS ON THE SUBJECT, THEY WERE IN THE BEREAVEMENT SECTION WITH SAD AND GLOOMY COLORS.

IT IS MY SINCERE HOPE THAT THIS JOURNAL MAY FILL IN THE GAP BETWEEN PREGNANCY AND BABY JOURNALS, SINCE NOT ALL PREGNANCIES END IN LIFE. MAY WE ALL HEAL AND LEARN TO REMEMBER OUR BABIES WITH PEACE, LOVE + ACCEPTANCE.

WWW.SWEETJULIAN.CO

Made in the USA
Columbia, SC
14 October 2024